YOUT... ......RY
WITH A TWIST

by Anthony Fouts

Published by
Church Growth Solutions
www.churchgrowthsolutions.com

Printed in the United States of America

ISBN 978-0-9817391-4-4

The insights in this study material are intended to better prepare individuals to be more effective leaders in building God's church.

Scriptures quotations are from the Holy Bible, King James Version (KJV) except where noted. Permission to quote from the Scriptures is acknowledged with appreciation.

Cover Design by
LifeLine Web Solutions
www.lifewebsolutions.com

Table of Contents

Discipleship with a Purpose should be taught as a companion manual to this book.

1.

Youth

Every great revival in history has had a strategic youth involvement!

God's promise for us is that in the last days *"I will pour my Spirit on your sons and daughters." (Acts 2:17)*

I firmly believe the world is experiencing a youth revolution. The question is: *Will the church step up to the challenge?* If the church does not go out and get them, the world will get them. This could well be the last opportunity to change our world. It's time for our Christian young people to take a stand for righteousness and claim their peers for eternity's sake. God wants young people who not only embody his name but reflect his character. Get into the action!

Greater is He that is <u>in you</u> than he that is in the world. (I John 4:4)

Studies have shown that the majority of people who are saved are saved before the age of 25. I think it would be smart to spend a major part of our energy on those who are the most receptive to the Gospel. Of those young people who reach the age of 18 *without accepting Christ as Savior,* nine out of 10 will spend eternity in Hell. The church must reach them while they are reachable!

Youth Attributes

1. Youth are at a place developmentally when they have more courage than fear.
2. Youth aren't locked in to outdated ways of thinking.
3. Youth have more freedom with their time and resources.
4. Youth have not lost their close tie between faith and emotions.
5. Youth love community and the *feeling* of being a part of a great cause.
6. Youth are intrigued with change.
7. Youth have a strong sense of justice.

Hype and enthusiasm may be a part of being young, but hype without substance soon dies for lack of an audience.
(A-quote)

Youth want a substance-based community that radiates life with enthusiasm.
(A-quote)

Give youth a program or they'll give you one. There is nothing that turns off our young people more than a boring youth program that leads them nowhere.

It's harder to *train in righteousness* than to *play at popularity.* Trendy methods and spiritual imitations of this world's culture do not produce strong disciples. This generation of young people has seen it all and is *ready for the real.* Young people are ready and waiting for *someone* to look past their facade and show genuine Christian love! You don't have to impress teenagers with hype or even high-tech stuff.

They have seen so much junk – even in the church – that many are hardened, but not too hard for God's love to break through.

The attacks against our youth we see today are just as deliberate as Satan's attempt to destroy Jesus or Moses as a child.

The enemy is aware that the seeds of deliverance for this generation could well be residing in the life of any one of the young people in your youth group.

The church must guard them well. Youth pastors must be vigilant!

Gangs are growing at unprecedented numbers. The church youth ministry can become their **gang** – their place to belong, their family, their place to identify with.

Young people will do almost anything to be part of a group that:

1. **Offers acceptance**
2. **Promotes a cause** they can believe in
3. **Demands boundaries**
4. **Allows for margins**

Successful youth leaders should memorize this list until it is burned into their brains.

Notes

4

2.

Recruit your Team

The most important part of youth ministry is not how well you minister to youth. Say what? Huh?

The most important ingredient of youth ministry is mentoring an ever-growing leadership team who will perpetuate your ministry even when you are away or dead. Without a substantial team of leaders, there's no possibility of reaching and impacting large numbers of young people. One person can only lead a small group of young people. Youth require too much time for one leader to do it all. Training adult leaders and older teenagers should be the constant goal of any successful youth ministry. Release your youth leaders in the power of the Holy Spirit!

In most churches, at least 40 percent of the uninvolved members would be willing to do some kind of ministry if asked and trained. Help is out there. Go get them!

The youth pastor should be the number one recruiter for ministry helpers.

Recruiting Process

Recruiting is one of the most important steps to any ministry.

One of the first things that Jesus, our example, did was to begin enlisting those men he would be training as disciples. They in turn would turn the world upside down. Men are recruited to a leader before they're committed to a cause. Before men will believe in your cause, they must first believe in you.

Contrary to popular belief, Jesus knew his disciples before he called them.

Jesus had lived in the same area all of his life. In a small town it would have been difficult not to know them. Jesus did not just burst on the scene and declare *"follow me."*

My suggestions from the example of Jesus

Make a list of people you have observed who may have the character and qualities you desire for leadership on your team. Look around the church during worship and see who is really worshipping. Watch how your prospective disciples interact with family and friends. Watch their reactions during the sermon.

Theses insights can tell you a lot about a person. Listen to the inner voice of the Holy Spirit. Only God knows the heart.

Begin to approach your prospective disciples one-on-one and ask for some time to talk with them.

Jesus recruited his team personally, one-on-one. Jesus did not advertise His ministry openings in the *Jerusalem Post* or the Jewish Sabbath bulletin.

Ask the prospective leader to give you their story. Have them give you the long version. Have them tell you about their life. Have them tell you their testimony and their experience with Christ. Listen for excuses. Excuses are usually lies to make someone look better. It is better to deal with potential problems in advance rather than to court disaster later on.

Tell them your story and the ministry that's in your heart. Watch their face to see if there is any indication that the Holy Spirit is dealing with them about the ministry that you're sharing with them. If you don't see fire in their eyes as you share your ministry, most likely this is not your person. This is not always true. Sometimes it takes awhile for the fire to kindle.

Ask them if they would be interested in the opportunity to join your ministry team and offer them training. Tell your prospective leader you're building a team and you will be training them. Let them know they will be working alongside you. Make this plain. People do not want to be placed in a position and then left hung out to dry.

Ask your prospective leader how they would feel about observing your ministry for a few weeks. Ask them to sit in on your next session, etc. Have at least two other prospective leaders joining you at this session also. This lets the prospective leader know they're not the only person you have asked.

This also lets the prospect know this is a very important ministry.

Meet with your prospective leader after about two weeks and ask them for a commitment of six months to one year.

Put them into a minor leadership role within the first three weeks – even if it's counting noses.

"Don't leave them standing around the wall, while you continue to do it all." (A-quote)

Continue to develop their skills and release more ministries to your new leaders.

Note: Ministry is more successful where team members enjoy being around each other. It's always a good idea to choose compatibility and desire for ministry over talent any day. Teamwork still makes the dream work! Remember it's not the size of the group you can gather around you, but rather the number of leaders you can release that will determine your success.

It generally takes one leader per 10 followers as a normal rule of thumb. Jesus chose 12 disciples. I'm just not that good yet and you definitely aren't. Ha!

When using the P.A.R.T.Y. concept, the only limit for how large your youth ministry can become is dependent only on how many leaders you can recruit and mentor.

The best practice in determining the size of a small group was modeled by Jesus. Jesus chose 12 men to disciple. He instructed us to follow what he had modeled. Leaders should be prepared to multiply their group into two groups whenever they consistently average 12 or more members in their groups.

Jesus told his disciples they should follow his example as a servant leader in John 12:15. *"For I have given you an example, that ye should do as I have done to you."*

We must remember that the whole life of Jesus was given for our example to follow, not just the humility of washing another's feet.

A good average size for a group to disciple would probably be from seven to 10 young people. It takes a very mature leader to be able to competently train 12 people at one time. In other words, if you want to have 200 young people in your youth ministry, then you will need to mentor about 25 new leaders. That may sound unrealistic, but the price of discipleship is not cheap. A perfect pattern for growth would be to have one leader in place for every five students. This equation allows room for growth.

Jesus gave us the perfect example on how to feed a multitude (a big event). He sat them down in small groups as helpers delivered to every group a sumptuous meal.

The Seesaw Effect

The seesaw effect of most youth group ministries is because there aren't enough leaders to mentor them.

Most young people come for their first visit to youth by the way of an invitation to a special event. While events are tremendous tools for young people to introduce their friends to their youth ministry, events are not meant for building strong relationships or developing discipleship.

There must be leadership in place to consolidate and mentor those who come to us. Many young people have come to our youth meetings and found closed doors for building relationships because there were no small groups or leaders to develop them.

These young people leave our churches and, more often than we care to admit, they are leaving their opportunity to know and serve Christ forever. We now have a generation of adults untouched by the church. Let's not make this mistake again.

The priority of youth ministry must focus on training leaders to disciple young people. Paul called them *"faithful men who will be able to teach others." (2 Timothy 2:2)*

There are no limits to the number you can disciple as long as you have a leader in place for every eight to 10 young people.

"This book of the law shall not depart from your mouth, but ye shall mediate on it day and night, so that you may be careful to do according to all that is written in it; for then you will make your way prosperous, and then you will have success." (Joshua 1:8-9 NASB)

I have seen many "Bright Star" youth pastors bite the dust because they thought they had to be "the Man."

I will say this so as to be unforgettable, not as mean as it might sound:

It is nothing short of stupid to think you can lead a large youth group by yourself.

Train servant leaders! Wise young youth pastors know what I am talking about.

The only viable strategy for reaching large numbers of young people is to mobilize middle schoolers, high schoolers and collegians to win their peers through small groups.

The very best method for reaching and discipling teenage peers is through some form of small group. The church must reach this generation in this generation!

Notes

3.

Boundaries

Healthy young people will always test the boundaries of their leadership or authority. This is why there should always be margins.

A margin is that blank space on the sides of a book page or letter. The margin is a safety zone that keeps the print from running off the page. Margins for young people allow room for grace and mercy to operate without losing them altogether while reining them back into the boundaries of the text they should be writing.

Teenagers ride a roller coaster of emotions and need your support, encouragement and unconditional love. Your frequent, strong affirmation will reassure your teenagers that you love and accept them.

I know many older people have given up on teenagers. They look at their dress, their lack of good manners and dismiss them as hopeless.

Teenagers are important to God!

They need someone to look past their outward appearance and really care about them. The key is to spend enough time with them to really get to know them.

Teen peer pressure is incredibly influential. Teenage years mark the natural time for beginning that breakaway from family and to express youthful individuality and independence. Their new relationships become a kind of *surrogate family* to them.

This is why it's so important to offer relationships within the boundaries of church ministries. Teenagers desperately need a safe social environment provided for them to participate in small groups. Your church small groups are a place where they can develop Christian buddies to fill the role of family away from family.

Teenagers are very open to spiritual things.

Teenagers are very open to spiritual things. This time in their lives is a very open door for a genuine personal relationship with God. Foundations of repentance, faith and living a separated life must be properly laid. Cults and occults have taken advantage of this opening for centuries. The church must step up to the challenge! The wind of youth revival is blowing. We can set our sails and go on the ride of our lives or we can hunker down and wait for the wind to subside to our normal status quo.

Two major things that influence a teenager: food and friends. Be a friend and feed them and you can win them. Simple, but true.

For older people who have a desire to reach young people, I offer the following suggestion. Hire them to do something for just an hour or so each week you can supervise. Offer them some refreshments and give them an opportunity to talk. This allows you time to get to know a wonderful young person and train them in a new skill. And this allows for you to get some things done around the house.

Just a note to remember

Teenagers crave sleep and often experience fatigue because of the physical developments their bodies are going through. This is not to be equated with laziness. Let them rest and they're usually full of energy once again.

Listen and don't criticize. Emotionally, they can change from one minute to the next. They're facing a flood of hormonal change. This is often the hardest part for older, mature adults to remember. Bear with them. It'll be amazing to see the relationships you can develop. These relationships often last a lifetime.

Younger believers need older friends willing to share their mature insights and experiences. Ask teenagers about their plans or how are they're doing in school. The Holy Spirit will give you discernment as to when and how to share Scripture or advice.

Notes

4.

Crowd Control for Events

Providing a big event night each month, or even quarterly, will help tie your youth hospitality homes into the total church body.

An annual youth extravaganza should probably be held during the Christmas vacation period.

One of the best ideas I have come up with for creating a disciplined atmosphere, especially for junior high event nights, is what I refer to as the *call to maturity.* I announce that everyone is so glad that such a wonderful group of young adults has decided to attend tonight. Then I acknowledge that I also realize they're at an awkward time of their lives where they'll struggle with immaturity. I announce the leadership team has an understanding heart toward this maturity challenge. I present the challenge for everyone to do their best to have a great time and if they should have a friend that gets too loud or is talking when they shouldn't, just gently touch them on the shoulder (positive peer pressure). After all, none of us have arrived yet.

End with: *"We all struggle with acting our age every now and then and I want you to know that no one is going to embarrass you because of* **a little immaturity on your part**. *Now let's have a great night!"*

Compliment the teenager two or three times throughout the evening on their attentiveness and maturity level to draw them back in if they're getting too out of hand.

This little speech seems to have miracle powers. Absolutely no teenage student wants to be identified as *immature in front of their peers.* The amazing thing is that I used this little speech so often the youth could quote it and correct me if I messed up and it still worked!

Events and productions draw crowds, but only small groups will bring about discipleship. Focus on training leaders and the numbers will come in due season.

5.

Age Division

One of the greatest challenges of a small youth group is the wide age range between the youngest and the oldest members in the group.

The age gap makes it very difficult to minister effectively to everyone in the group. The younger members are expected to "get what you can" while the more mature often feel bored without a challenge. Twelve year olds do not belong with nineteen year olds.

If you have 10 youths in your group, I recommend you recruit a leader helper for half of your group by age grade.

The sooner youth are divided into grade- and age-appropriate groups, the faster your youth group will grow and the greater the opportunity for discipleship.

For example:

Group 1: 12 and 13 year olds

Group 2: 14, 15 and 16 year olds

Group 3: 17 and 18 year olds

Group 4: 18 (out of high school) and 19 year olds

For worship, I recommend youth groups be divided into junior high and senior high when the group reaches about 50 in attendance.

If you divide the worship into smaller groups too soon, you lose the dynamics of group worship.

I strongly recommend a different service be provided for the core group where worship and training are on a higher level, if not weekly, then at least monthly.

For training, the more divisions you can produce with six to eight students in each group, the more discipleship will take place and the greater opportunity for leadership to be developed among the students. Age-division grouping is often done in successful churches through Sunday school age division classes. A Search Institute study has found that only 11 percent of churchgoing teenagers have a well-developed faith.[1] We must do better.

Many youth pastors make the mistake of only developing the older teenagers to be leaders. I recommend leadership development begin in junior high. If you begin to recruit junior high students for leaders, they'll be strong young leaders by the time they're seniors. Senior student leaders should be recruiting their own leadership teams! Responsibility comes with privilege.

6.

P.A.R.T.Y. Ministry Concept

He saw a publican named Levi sitting at the receipt of custom: and He said unto him, Follow me. (Luke 5:29)

Luke gives a powerful illustration of a newly called disciple named Levi (Matthew) opening up his home for a party with all his old Roman tax collector buddies (Publicans).

And he left all, rose up, and followed him.

And Levi made Him a great feast in his own house: and there was a great company of publicans and of others that sat down with them.

But their scribes and Pharisees murmured against His disciples, saying; Why do ye eat with publicans and sinners?

And Jesus answering said unto them; They that are whole need not a physician; but they that are sick.

I came not to call the righteous, but sinners to repentance. (Luke 5:29,32)

Teach the scriptural patterns, but give your young people practical life application to the Scriptures. Faith without works (corresponding action) is fantasy.

Young people must learn how to transfer Scripture into practical daily application.

A P.A.R.T.Y. is hosted by a spiritually mature adult who has had training and understands young people along with a mature teenage leader (s) as cohost.

The requirements for leadership as a hospitality home leader are the same as other departmental leaders in the church.

P. A. R. T. Y.

This is a small group strategy for youth to develop spiritual maturity while bringing their unchurched friends into a fun, non-confrontational atmosphere where Jesus is presented in a fun, yet spiritual dimension.

It's much easier for a teenager to invite someone to a party than to a church service or youth service. Young people often survive in a large worship service but they thrive in small groups. As relationships are developed and Christ is honored, church attendance will provide a more positive enrichment for them.

P. Putting God first

A. A passionate desire for souls

R. Reaching our peers

T. Taking our city

Y. Youth with a vision

Youth aren't much different than they have always been. They have many of the same basic needs.

1. Youth want to be affirmed

2. Youth want to follow a leader who practices what they teach.

3. Youth want a bigger-than-life challenge.

4. Youth want to be treated with respect.

5. Youth desire spiritual reality.

6. Youth want to be acknowledged as mature young adults.

7. Youth want to be loved.

Development

P. = Putting God first. Youth will learn the basic Bible doctrines with fun and enthusiasm while getting instructions on *the how to* of having a daily devotional life.

A. = A passionate desire for other souls. Youth offer daily prayer for unchurched peers.

R. = Reaching our peers. Youth inviting their peers to a party

T. = Taking our city. Youth developing hospitality homes all over the area!

Y. = Youth with a vision. Youth reaching youth throughout the world and are maturing into adulthood when they will one day open their own home as a hospitality home.

You may want to use alternative words if party has a negative connotation in your area. In some places party may be associated with the use of alcohol or marijuana. Names such as The Connection, Gathering or just Event may be your ticket.

The party starts as a hospitality home open for a couple of hours a week for young people to hang out in a Christian atmosphere.

It takes place in the home of anyone willing to open their home and hearts to host a small gathering of young people for two hours a week. This can be young couples or senior adults and everyone in between.

The most successful host homes are generally held in the homes of Christian parents with teenagers.

Parents of teenagers often involve other parents with teenagers. This helps to enlarge your circle of leadership. The key for hosting a hospitality home is to really love and understand young people.

As you minister and interact with young people, it's important that you are alert to their need to be accepted and their consciousness of self-image. Teenagers are constantly evaluating their relationships with other teens. It's a very uncertain and insecure time in their maturity. They need confirmation from you as their leader.

Host/hostess responsibilities

- Pray.
- Be sensitive to the young people's spiritual needs.

- Have the living area and bathrooms guest ready.

- Have light refreshments ready. Remember that teens are ravenous.

- Set a time schedule that both the parents and young people are made aware of.

- Have appropriate music playing most of the time; you may want the music cranked up a little at times.

The P.A.R.T.Y. Program

- Start with the food and the drinks, preferably in the kitchen. Hang out.

- Provide games, puzzles, brainteasers or videos to keep them busy for about an hour. Hang out.

- Have a mature Christian young person prepared to give an eight- to 12-minute devotional or testimony. Provide materials if they need them.

- Prayer time should follow as appropriate.

- Alternate the speakers weekly, if possible.

- Eventually use all the young people to share a devotional or a testimony. This builds their faith and confidence along with their leadership skills.

- Close on time.

- As they leave, say something affirming and invite them back.

There may be many instances where a leader may feel called to work with the youth ministry and has a great understanding of young people but doesn't have the financial means to host a party.

Remember there is a wealth of people who don't feel called to youth ministry but who will gladly provide refreshments if only they were asked. *You have not because you ask not.* Don't leave out the senior adults in this area of your ministry or your neighbors either.

If God has given you the vision, God also has the provision. You may have to go and ask for it. Many stores and restaurants are often supporters of youth functions. Don't be afraid to share your vision and present your need and boldly ask for their help. We are never beggars, but at the same time we should never be ashamed to ask for help for such a worthy cause. People will give to a good cause. There is no greater cause than our youth.

7.

Creative Ideas for Hospitality Homes

*These games may sound silly and
unsophisticated, but young people want safe,
fun relationships over sophistication any day.*

This is why I inserted them. You don't have to
break the bank every week to have a successful
youth ministry.

Mexican Fiesta

Decorate with bright colors such as turquoise,
yellow, orange etc. a piñata would certainly add
to the festivities. The host/hostess may want to
wear a sombrero.

Suggested food: Tortilla chips and salsa with
bean dip and soft drinks.

Games: Mexican bean pitch.

Everyone receives a large dried bean (lima).
Each player will mark his or her bean with a
marker to be able to identify it. Some will be
quite creative in their artwork. The object of the
game is to toss it as close to a masking tape
line as possible without going over.

To land on the line or be the closest to the line
without going over produces a winner! There
should be prizes of Mexican candy, etc. Always
allow for a tie. This should be repeated several
times.

27

This can be changed to toss the bean into a sombrero. You just allow a little more distance to the target. Girls and guys may want to have teams or even do it separately. Have fun.

The devotional may consist of learning Spanish words for God, Holy Spirit, Jesus, etc.

Freely use greetings such as *hola* or *buenos dias* along with *señor* and *señorita*.

Pizza party

Order plenty of pizza and soda. Show a good video.

Devotional: Use something to relate to a Godly character.

Karaoke night

This is really fun time. Have lots of music available. This can be hilarious but dangerous to young egos. Tell everyone to watch his or her comments.

8.

Rules of the House

1. Show respect toward the host/hostess, leaders and others.

2. No open show of affection.

3. Remember the six-inch rule. No closer to each other than six inches.

4. No roughhousing.

5. Help with clean up. Help them learn responsibility.

6. No unkind or foul language.

7. Don't take what isn't yours.

8. In other words, act as mature young adults.

9. Hang out, talk, and eat – the holy trinity of a successful youth gathering.

10. Wear modest apparel; no showing of underwear or wearing skimpy clothes. (Remember margins.)

11. Arrive and leave on schedule.

Believe it or not, young people want guidelines and boundaries.

The Rules of the House should be implemented for every youth event from youth camp to skate night. No exceptions!

Rules and boundaries free young people to have fun and enjoy their time at youth service.

Boundaries are not a negative concept, except for those who are there for the purpose of disrupting. Boundaries protect everyone.

Love and affirmation is easier to dispense than discipline. Both are required if you really love young people. Love requires discipline and confrontation when following the pattern of Jesus.

Jesus confronted the rich young ruler. He did not lower his standards to make adjustments for him because he was young or wealthy. *(Matthew 19:16-22)*

Jesus rescued the woman caught in adultery but also admonished her to turn from her sinful lifestyle. *(John 8:1-11)*

Youth leaders must be ready to confront error, affirm and love unconditionally, while standing on the truth of God's word without compromise!

The Consequences for Ignoring the Rules of the House

It's useless to have rules of the house if there is no consequence for deliberant defiance of the rules. I also believe that all of us – especially teenagers – need margins to allow for the grace of God to work and hopefully to get back on the right page.

Every student should be given a form with the Rules of the House listed, along with the consequences for defiance printed on the reverse side.

This should be given to every student to read and sign as a form of enrollment. They need to understand there are clear boundaries. They can feel safe and have fun in an exclusive party. Only those who pledge to honor the rules are here.

For the first offense

I recommend a margins warning with a reminder to the student of their previous pledge to honor the rules of the house.

For the second offense

I recommend the offender be quietly escorted to another room by a mature leader of the same sex for counseling and an opportunity for repentance.

If there's a truly repentant attitude, the student is allowed to quietly return to the group after a pat on the shoulder or hug.

If the student is defiant of the authority, he will be kept from the group until his parents can retrieve him. The student and the parent together are instructed of the seriousness of the offense and cannot return until there has been an attitude adjustment or no less than one week's absence.

For the third offense

I recommend the offender be quietly escorted to another room for an opportunity to repent. They are reminded they have made their decision to dishonor the rules of the house and you must be honest to honor their decision with the consequences. They will not be able to return to the group for three weeks and only after meeting with the senior pastor and bringing a note from him recommending their reinstatement.

For a fourth offense,

I recommend the student be quietly escorted to another room and the parents called to retrieve them. The parents will be notified that the student will not be able to return to the group for at least six months and that counseling is recommended. Love is firm.

A group will not grow without boundaries. Young people need loving boundaries with well-defined margins.

9.

Communication Is More Than Important

Electronically copy every sermon or teaching for your protection and personal reference. The way youth services get communicated to parents is not always in the context it actually played out.

Every parent deserves a monthly update letter, card, email, note on a paper napkin – something to communicate what's going on in the youth group and in their young person's life in particular. The door of communication should be taken off its hinges when it comes to youth ministry and just leave it open. A no closed doors policy in youth ministry is a safety net policy.

When your cause is spelled out clearly and your strategy is in operation, it becomes easy to say, *"This is what we are about and this is what we are doing."* This gives parents and other leaders a sense of security and pride – as well as keeping you on track.

Your cause will give you the openness to say no to those who want to impose their ideas into your ministry.

This is not in opposition to the God-ordained ideas you will need as your group evolves. Your cause statement provides a safety net of integrity against those harebrained ideas so many youth groups are noted for.

There are vast multitudes of young people waiting for a leader who will inspire them to follow.

Will it be a man of God with fire in his bones or another Hitler with his hordes of Brownshirts who will attempt to control and destroy the world?

There's an army of young people out there waiting for a leader to step up with their marching orders. Will it be you?

Notes

10.

The Cause

*The market for a cause to believe in is infinite.
Millions of young people are waiting and looking
for something and somebody to believe in.*

Young David said, *"Is there not a cause?"* when
he was faced with the plight of the Israelite
army cowering before Goliath.

Young people hunger for a worthy cause.
Boring, ill-prepared programs with no direction
will not suffice for this modern generation.

The development of a healthy youth ministry
demands a cause. I want to list six causes I feel
are the Biblical ground zero for any youth
ministry. You may want to refer to your cause
as a Quest or Purpose.

List one:

1. Hanging out together

2. Learning Scripture for practical life
   application

3. Sharing their faith

4. Talking to God about everything

5. Loving God all the time

6. Making a difference in the world

You may want to use terms such as:

1. Fellowship

2. Discipleship

3. Evangelism

4. Prayer or Intersession

5. Worship

6. Ministry

This second list doesn't often have much meaning for unchurched young people even though they mean the same thing.

Whatever you determine to be on your list of principles should also be printed in every youth publication.

Your cause should be listed in every printout or email used for youth ministry. Every leader should be able to quote *the cause* at a moment's notice. Young people want to know they have a cause with a strategy to carry it out.

Put up posters with your *CAUSE* printed boldly on it. Declare it. *"We have a Cause!"*

You may want to list only three or four principles. Whatever you do, do not have more than seven principles to memorize or the excitement of your cause may become drudgery.

After you've determined what your cause is going to be comprised of, move on to the next step.

Step number two is to teach from the Scriptures **WHY this is our cause.**

1.   Hanging out – Acts 2:42, etc.

2.   Learning Scripture – 2 Timothy 2:15, etc.

3.   Sharing – Matthew 28:19, etc.

4.   Talking to God – Philippians 4:6, I Thessalonians 5:17, Luke 18:1, etc.

5.   Loving God – Psalms 95:6. Philippians 3:3, etc.

6.   Making a difference – Mark 16:15, etc.

When your young people began to live out the cause, even parents begin to be supportive. Miracles still happen!

There are times of necessity when a youth pastor must address subjects such as drugs, promiscuity, foul language, etc. Dealing with problems will never end in a youth ministry, but to constantly address problems sends a wrong message to the young people and they will not mature spiritually in the Word. STAY with your cause and when absolutely necessary, address problems in the context of your cause.

Build teenagers in the cause of Christ and many of their problems will be overcome by the Holy Spirit applying the Word to their heart. Preach the Gospel. Stay with the program.

Don't change your message every time a problem arises or you will never mature your group. Satan loves to keep us sidetracked and off-center with problems in the youth group.

Most problems should be addressed privately and personally, not publicly. Stay focused and on track!

There is no need to gather a crowd of unruly teenagers when you haven't established a core group of spiritually strong young people. Research studies have shown that only 11 percent of churchgoing teenagers have a well-developed faith.[1] Build a strong core group first and they will enlarge your borders as they share their faith with their circle of influence. Discipleship is more about training than just trying.

I have seen far too many youth ministries destroyed by bringing in too many unchurched teenagers too soon. Promiscuity, drugs, foul language and stealing are not strangers to some youth groups. There can be a significant difference between a youth group and a youth ministry. There are churches that could be reaching and teaching thousands of young people but are bogged down by a handful of troubled young people.

Get the troubled young people professional ministry help then go reach the thousands you are qualified to reach. You aren't doing the troubled teenager or yourself a favor by trying to minister outside your calling. Love is kind, but love also operates in wisdom.

Youth ministry is not about building a crowd, but about building the church of Jesus Christ.

Young people with special needs and problems need special care by qualified ministry programs, not a regular church youth group. Satan has duped many a well-meaning youth leader into thinking that he's acting in love by bringing the problem teenager into his youth group. He or she in turn destroys everything that is holy and righteous.

The good shepherd cares for and protects his sheep. Leave the big problems to a qualified "Moses" who can handle them.

The Scripture instructs us to be wise. That is the opposite of stupid – in which I have seen some bad cases.

I realize that I am coming on strong, but I have seen far too many churches and youth ministries destroyed in the name of compassion and love, etc. It's time to build an army of Godly young people using God's method and change the world they're capable of changing.

Ministers – whether youth or senior pastor – are only required to minister within the realm of their calling and giftedness. God did not call us to reach everyone.

The next time you decide to operate outside of your calling and giftedness, please remember a bad case of stupid takes a long time to recover from and takes a lot more than antibiotics to heal. (See the section on target audience in my book *Locating your Harvest.*)

If you are called to work with troubled young people, more power to you. Get all the training you can get and don't let anything stop you.

I recommend you seek out a large church with a good accountability program for your spiritual covering.

Notes

11.

Sharing Your Faith

Young people are generally very reluctant to share their faith with a stranger.

The method that seems most successful is to train them to share Christ within their own circle of relationships.

Here is a list of mini-steps that you might want to challenge them with.

1. Share with your friends that you have accepted Christ as your savior.

2. Invite your unchurched friends to a P.A.R.T.Y.

3. Share with your small group

4. Share with your unchurched friends why you are a Christian.

5. Share with your unchurched friends how you became a Christian.

6. Share with your friends Christ whenever the Holy Spirit directs you. They will be ready to receive Him!

7. Enlarge your circle of relationships.

Every Christian young person in your group should have a copy of this list in their wallet or purse.

Have this list printed on business cards and hand them out regularly.

Young people lose things. It may take some of your group a whole semester to even get to number three. That's ok; keep on keeping on. Let them share before the group each time they have applied a new level. It will inspire the others. Make a big thing about their accomplishments. Clap, have a drum roll, flash the lights. It's a big thing for a young person to share their faith.

Remember Paul's instructions on how to talk to unbelievers: *"Let your conversation be always full of grace, seasoned with salt, so that you may know how to answer everyone."* *(Colossians 4:6)*

Our goal is to love a person into the kingdom of God, not to win a religious debate. (A-quote)

A second card that your young people should have is their unchurched friends list. This can also be printed on the back of the sharing card. These cards can be purchased at your local office supply and printed on your computer.

My friend list:

1._____
2._____
3._____
4._____
5._____

Teach your young people to pull this card out every day and to repeat each name before God asking for their friend's salvation. It is amazing to see what happens to your problems whenever you pray for others.

The six steps listed above are to be taught repeatedly with consistency. Teach these principles in every way possible. Use drama, illustrated sermons, PowerPoint, videos and games. Christian young people deserve the best training possible on how to share Christ.

Teenagers need to know how to articulate and defend their faith!

Notes

Notes

12.

Youth in Ministry

Let youth minister.

Well-trained, well-dressed, smiling, polite teenagers will impress even the hardest souls. Note: All of the above adjectives are important.

Youth in ministry is a great discipleship tool and lots of fun for young people.

Youth Greeters

Youth greeters are one of the greatest assets of a growing church. Visiting parents of teenagers are always impressed to see young people serving in a public ministry position. This is one area of ministry that must have youth involvement.

General Benefits

- It helps them to develop people skills.

- They get respect from adults and peers alike.

- They develop a sense of self confidence.

- They learn the feel of real ministry.

- Life skills are fine-tuned.

They should be rotated to allow as many youth to participate as possible.

A good adult leader can be very effective in the Christian development of your young people.

Youth Ministry in the Children's Department:

Without a doubt, this is one of the greatest tools for learning discipleship principles for leadership, parenting, general ministry and life skills. A very skilled young minister stated this bit of wisdom: *"If you can keep the attention of children and youth, you can speak anywhere."*

- They can enroll new students.

- They can be greeters and ushers.

- They can help tell the Bible sermon.

- Clowning is a powerful ministry tool for reaching all ages, especially those in the children's department.

- They can provide music.

- Teenagers are excellent puppeteers.

- They can lead worship.

- They can provide tech support with lighting, videos, DVDs, etc.

- They can help with clean up.

- They learn discipline through weekly meetings for training and encouragement. All of this accelerates ministry and life skills.

- They are required to be disciplined in daily Scripture reading, prayer and dress to be on the team.

- They must be a part of the planning process.

- Youth helpers in the children's department provide a tremendous opportunity for discipleship training for themselves as well the children.

Service Projects

Service projects are excellent tools to train young people about servant ministry. Teenagers will often sign up for a service project over a trip to Six Flags. I haven't figured this out yet, but I think it's because the feeling they get from helping someone is greater than the joy of an outing. Wonders never cease.

Many service projects can be done by young people with adult supervision.

1. Remodeling the youth room.

2. Grounds projects.

3. Inner-city church repairs.

4. Mowing grass for the elderly or single moms.

5. Shoveling snow in winter for the elderly.

6. Oil changes for single parents and those who could use a break is a great learning experience for the boys when supervised by a good mechanic.

7. Cleaning windshields is a power tool to display love. Go to a parking lot of a grocery or retail chain or auto parts house and clean windshields while leaving a business card from the church youth department.

I strongly recommend quarterly service projects be an important addition to your youth ministry. Servant ministry is a vital training tool for young disciples.

Service projects teach young people skills and cooperation but most of all, they learn to feel what it's like to be a part of a ministry team ministering to the needs of others. Youth ministries that only entertain and offer no real-life opportunities for service are doing a disservice to their youth. A major part of serving Christ is serving others. No matter how small your youth group may be, plan a service project.

I know of one church that built a huge ministry around cleaning public toilets for businesses. They now have a church full of service-minded businessmen and women.

Short-Term Mission Trips

I firmly believe that every Christian young person should participate in at least one mission trip to another country and culture. Yearly short-term mission trips should be a part of the yearly calendar of every youth ministry. Living in Texas has given me the opportunity to lead several mission trips into Mexico. Wherever you live, there should be annual short-term mission trip to another country.

Most small churches join other churches to make their missions trip happen. Youth leaders, who have never been on a mission trip before and don't know where to start, can begin by calling larger churches in the area or the denominational headquarter of denominations with a similar belief structure. Thousands of churches send out mission teams every year.

Some churches have opted to do inner-city missions in some of America's larger cities where they can experience other cultures. Don't think that American inner cities are safer than a foreign country.

The same security precautions should be taken as though you were in a foreign country. This is coming from someone who has lived near Dallas for several years.

Whatever you do, always go with a seasoned veteran who speaks the language of the country you will be visiting. I have also had some not-so-good experiences of poorly planned mission trips. Plan your mission trip well with someone who has recently led a successful mission to the country or inner city you plan to visit.

It doesn't always set well with parents for your church youth group to return home from their mission trip with one their teenagers missing in action. That was meant for a little comic relief, but this is one area of ministry you should take very seriously.

Drama Teams

Interpretive dance and tambourine is often integrated into effective drama performances as well as clowning. A ministering drama team should be the goal of every youth ministry. Drama is a powerful tool to minister the Gospel and to teach discipleship.

Mission projects are much more effective when presenting the Gospel through drama, clowning and mime – especially when the audience doesn't speak your language. Drama helps young people express their faith in a way that not only ministers to others but also enriches their own faith. Costumes and make-up encourages even the shyest young person to become a bold witness for Christ.

There are many opportunities for your youth to present their talent as well as a message of hope *from local malls to the mission field.* Daycares and nursing homes offer excellent opportunities to perform and minister. Many junior high and high schools will allow assembly time for a well-prepared drama on the perils of drug and alcohol use.

Whoever prepares your mission trip agendas should always inquire about the possibility of school assemblies. I have some powerful reports of salvations and healings after a simple Gospel drama presentation at a school in Guatemala.

There are also very few things that will touch the heart of the local church family more than to see their young people minister before the church body in a drama or to hear the positive reports of their ministry.

Many high schools and local colleges offer classes in drama at little or minimal cost. There are also schools of Christian clowning. I recommend someone on your team check it out. This ministry can impact many for Christ.

I want to reiterate the importance of a ministering drama team! Do it. Do it with prayer. Do it with anointing. Do it with style! Do it with excellence! Do it as unto the Lord. This may open up an even greater door of opportunity.

Performing Music

Every young person with an ounce of musical talent should be encouraged to develop it to their fullest extent. Music is the language that exceeds cultural barriers and speaks to the heart. It's so important that young people be exposed to quality Christian music – the earlier the better. Public schools often provide quality music programs. While few of them provide training for Christian music, our young people can have the benefit of their training and use it for Christ!

There are many talented students in public school music programs who have no venue to express their musical talents. The church can become a training ground for exposing these talented students to Christian music and the Christ of the music. Don't be afraid to invite musically talented young people to join your youth worship team for a jam session. God works in mysterious ways.

Those young people in your group who have shown a serious interest in worship ministry should be invited to join the main auditorium worship team or band on occasion.

Who knows what God may be up to next! There are youth worship teams and bands that are serving all over America, making an impact for Christ! It burdens my heart to visit a church where the young people are worshiping with an older adult band or CD player when I know there are scores of talented youth who should be there playing and ministering for God. I salute those young people who come faithfully regardless of the obstacles. I pray for the day that even the smallest churches have a quality Christian band and worship team.

Notes

13.

Soul-Winning Teams

The Lord is not slack concerning his promises, as some men count slackness, but is longsuffering to us-ward, not willing that any should perish, but that all should come to repentance. (2 Peter 3:9)

Any good youth group should have a soul-winning team or teams. These are your Green Beret troops. They should be trained in Scripture to effectively lead anyone to a personal relationship in Christ. To have a soul-winning team is one of the most important decisions you will make as youth leader. Challenge everyone to be a part of this frontline offensive.

Teenagers do not need to learn 15 different methods to become a soul winner. A few basic Scriptures and a simple method can have your teenagers winning souls.

Steps to Starting

1. Teach your teenagers the basic Romans Road method of witnessing.

2. Have them mark in their Bibles the following scriptures: Romans 3:10, 3:23, 6:23, 5:8, 10:9,10 and 10:13.

3. Have each teenager write in the margin of their Bible where the next Scripture is found.

In the margin of Romans 3:10 would be written 3:23 and beside Romans 3:23 would be 6:23.

4. After this exercise is completed, I suggest they begin to memorize each Scripture and add one new Scripture weekly.

Other good soul-winning scriptures would be Ephesians 4:8, 9 or I John 1: 8, 9, etc.

In a few weeks, your group should begin practicing on winning each other.

Pair them up and pick a lost sinner from their team to "win."

This practice is a great deal of fun and causes some sincere soul searching for everyone. This practice should be repeated often. Training your teenagers to be soul winners will be the best thing you will ever do for them. This is not a one-time event but a weekly lifestyle of going out to reach the lost. Clear the calendar and set a time. Do it every week, rain or shine!

Wednesday before regular service time may be a good time and place to get started. Some churches have the teenage soul winners come early and eat together before going out before church. This is a good time to invite prospects for Wednesday night youth group.

Getting Started in Soul-Winning

Getting started is the hardest part of any journey. I do not advocate you send your teenagers out on a street corner where they will try pulling someone into conversation. I am not opposed to that either.

I recommend you begin a prospect list from all of the unchurched friends and acquaintances from the members of your group. This would be a great place to start visiting.

The Plan

Just drop by a prospect's house for a quick visit with your team consisting of a leader and two young soul winners. Use only guy teams and girl teams.

Never use co-ed teams. This tends to lead to boyfriend and girlfriend challenges.

Simply invite your prospective person to church or youth group and see where the Holy Spirit wants to take the conservation. Then and only then do I suggest that you go any further. God has some people prepared and ready to receive and others just need to be watered with love and concern.

Picking fruit before it's ripe usually leads to loss.

The more teenagers go out soul winning, the higher their confidence level becomes.

Encourage them to not only go out as a team effort but to become a soul winner everywhere they go. Because of the fervor of young people, God has used teens in every great revival in history. Many times young people were the catalyst for the revival movement.

I anticipate over the next few years, youth ministries that primarily stay in an entertainment mode of just hype and fun will lose many of their strong young people to churches that provide a spiritual challenge. Students who have a heart for God will move toward a challenge wherever they can find it. Provide the challenge and keep them!

Keep Soul Winning Going

Keeping your teams enthused and excited is a big deal. Winning souls because you're supposed to has a way of becoming old hat to most everyone, including teenagers.

One of the most effective means of creating a continuous momentum is to have each team set annual goals for the number of souls they intend to reach. Review their progress toward that annual goal in every monthly meeting.

Goals set too low don't present a challenge or create excitement.

Goals set too high are tickets to failure. Help each team set realistic goals.

Each team will compete against their goal, not against another team. Post these goals in the youth room and refer to them frequently. A prize should be given for the student who brings the most people into the youth group or church.

One teenager won to Christ may bring in four or five other people, including their parents, friends or siblings.

To keep enthusiasm going, I recommend your soul-winning teams choose a good team name for the total group and names for each witnessing team. This helps to identify each team as well as promote friendly competition. All team names must meet staff approval. One group that I am aware of call themselves "The Fishermen's Club." I don't know how the girls felt or if they cared. The point is to pick a good name that everyone can identify with in a positive manner.

Encourage your soul winners to tell their stories to the rest of the group and include some of their testimonies into the Sunday morning service. Casual church members need to see what it's like for young people to be on fire for Christ.

Fired up young people have a way of burning into an all-church revival.

Personal Conduct

Conduct should always be exemplary. No horseplay or teasing. Stay off the grass. Walk on the walks or driveway. Be careful what you say when approaching a house. Some people can read lips.

Wear church attire when representing your church as a soul winner. Modesty is the word. There are laws in place in Dallas and other cities against showing your underwear. This is not only illegal, but also immodest.

All clothes need to be neat and clean.

Breath mints will help you be nonoffensive.

Get Ready, Get Ready

1. Mark and memorize the Romans Road. (Romans 3:10, 3:23, 6:23, 5:8, 10:9-10, 10:13)

2. Practice winning your friends, and go over your presentation by yourself until you can see yourself doing soul winning.

3. Make sure to map your Scriptures in the margin so you can follow them even when you're nervous.

4. Pray for the Holy Spirit to lead and empower you.

5. Make sure your checklist includes a New Testament, pen, tracts and information cards.

Presenting the Gospel: Ten Steps

1. Smile. Begin with a warm greeting and a compliment. Compliment something that seemed obvious as you came up to the door. The lawn, the dog, the neighborhood are all possibilities. Talk clearly and in a normal voice. People tend to talk faster, louder and with a higher pitch when nervous.

2. Introduce yourself and your partner and say where you are from. At the same time give them a tract, a church business card or both to the prospect.

3. Ask them if they attend church anywhere. Be complimentary if they go to a good church. Ask if they would consider visiting your church sometime, but only if you suspect they aren't sincere or are unhappy with their church.

4. Ask how they're doing in their spiritual journey.

5. If their response is that they could certainly use improvement, follow up with: "Are you sure about your spiritual destiny?"

6. The Holy Spirit will lead you as to whether you should present the Scriptures.

   - *Everyone has sinned. (Romans 3:10, 23)*

   - *There is a price for sin. (Romans 6:23)*

   - *Jesus has paid the price for sin. (Romans 5:8)*

   - *Accept Christ by faith. (Romans 10:9, 10, 13)*

7. Lead them in a prayer of repentance.

8. Congratulate them and pray a blessing over them, including a review of some of the Scriptures you just covered.

9. Encourage them to be with you in church on Sunday; fill out an enrollment card for them to sign and offer to have someone pick them up.

10. Contact them again before Sunday.

Enrollment Cards

Youth enrollment cards are a powerful tool to encourage young people or anyone, for that matter, to attend a church youth group after verbally committing to attend. After you get their vital information (name, phone, etc.), simply give it to them to sign. There is something about signing anything that makes it much more serious. Your chances of a prospect following through with their commitment are almost doubled by the prospect signing their name.

A lot of times, the devil will steal the new commitment before the prospect can get to church. A signature seems to seal the deal more effectively. I don't necessarily understand this, but it works anyway. It's not something to be taken lightly.

A soul-winning team that consistently goes out at least 40 times in the year (giving time off for holidays and vacation) will see phenomenal growth. This can create some interesting logistical challenges. I am aware of one church (ours) that had to surrender the main auditorium on Wednesday for the revival that was happening in the Wednesday night youth service. The youth outgrew their youth room.

The greatest thing is to see the growth in your team members. I strongly recommend that every youth ministry have a strong soul-winning emphasis.

14.

Godly Connections

There is much to gain by communication in an open and caring manner.

The goal of conversation is to connect with people and the world around us. Horizons are broadened and opportunities are expanded and relationships are deepened and become more meaningful as you connect with those around you.

Begin by opening your mind and attitudes to those around you. You don't have to compromise your values or lower your standards to love someone as they are. God loves you with all of your imperfections and God's people need to do the same with others.

Building new relationships is not about pushing others to see your point of view. Relationships are about communicating the love of Christ. The church can no longer afford to be represented as an evangelistic "swat team."

A great part of communicating the love of Christ is to listen carefully to those you are attempting to build relationships with. Set a goal today to make contact with others outside your present circle of relationships.

Communicating

Body language is our nonverbal communication. Does our way of standing, walking, gesturing or our body posture communicate to others? The answer is yes!

61

Our body language communicates our feelings and attitudes long before we speak.

Research has show that 70 percent of communication is nonverbal.

Of our verbal communication, only seven percent is communicated by the words actually spoken, while a large percentage of our words are perceived by the tone of our voice.[1]

Our level of receptivity to others is portrayed by our physical language long before verbal conversation ever begins. You will be judged quickly by the first signals you give off. It's vitally important Christians present a warm, friendly, positive first impression.

Paul said, *"...I bring my body under subjection..." (1 Corinthians 9:27)* and we must do the same.

There may be a person whose physical or perhaps even spiritual condition is repulsive to us who certainly don't need to see our body language saying, *"I don't want to be here."*

I have personally observed Christians attempting to give a witness for Christ who spoke mountains about not really caring with their body language while communicating the Gospel with their tongue. The recipient knew they were witnessing out of duty and not from a caring heart.

A Pleasant Smile

A pleasant smile is the best indicator of an open, caring attitude.

"Smile and the whole world smiles with you," someone once wrote into a song.

It's true that most people will return a smile when it's freely given away. Try it. You may like it. A smile sends out friendly messages that say, "I approve of you." It is just the reverse of a frown.

I have heard people say, *"I just feel comfortable standing or sitting this way."* This usually means they stand or sit with their arms folded or refuse to make steady eye contact or their hand is always near their mouth. My answer to you is life is not all about your comfort. And as a Christian, you need to represent Christ and not yourself. Learn and practice how to present yourself and Christ in a positive light.

A Few Suggestions

When listening to someone always lean forward slightly and nod your head. Now that wasn't so hard, was it?

Always couple eye contact with a friendly smile. Direct eye contact is the strongest of the nonverbal gestures. This doesn't mean a constant stare. Staring someone down definitely communicates a particular message. I hope that's not your message.

Give a warm handshake. Start and end a conversation with a firm, friendly handshake. There is great power in the human touch.

Friendships are like plants; they can grow slowly and steadily with time and with the proper nourishment can really amaze us. Many people out there are your potential friends and you can develop relationships with them!

Developing relationships takes time, effort, commitment, give-and-take and a lot of Godly tolerance for the human failures we all posses.

Notes

15.

Tools for the Ministry

Jesus used a boat to row out into the water where his voiced would be reflected and amplified from the water so that all could hear.

That Scripture gives us a clear example of the use of tools to perform a better job of getting the Gospel out. Churches should use every tool available to get their message out. Jack Hyles gave us this great quote: *"Fish with a trotline, put every hook in the water you can get."*[1] (A trotline is a fishing line with as many as a hundred hooks.)

A youth pastor preached a dynamic message on reaching the unchurched, concluding with an emotional alter appeal. The response was charged with emotions and tears of repentance. The following week a few of the members made a feeble attempt to witness to others. The rest of the members just felt guilty and returned the following week.

Another youth pastor preached a fair message on reaching the unchurched and concluded by handing out cards to write down the names and addresses of five to10 unchurched neighbors or friends. They were instructed to bring their cards back the following Wednesday so they could be copied for the Thursday night prayer teams, which would join them in praying for their unchurched friends.

He then reiterated how to show acts of kindness to their unchurched friends as well as pray for each of them by name. He provided the tool and the plan.

Which group do you think will grow?

Small groups, Net Sundays, visitors cards, computers, email, microphones, lighting, prayer cards and enrollment cards are all tools to help us perform our ministry. Buildings are tools; buses and vans are tools.

There is nothing sacred about buildings or buses; they're just sticks and stones and iron or plastic. The church should have and use the finest tools available to present God's message to this end-time generation! Fish with a trotline!

Double Your Youth Center

Your youth center, youth room or wherever you meet should represent your church and God well. This investment tool for the future is worth the effort. Paint, carpet, lighting, décor and sound should be given special care.

If you are planning to build a new campus or youth center, double the size of your youth and children's department. At the time of this writing (2007), this is one of the critical areas creating a bottleneck, preventing church growth. If there isn't a decent place for the kids, the parents won't be coming back.

A youth revolution is here. Get ready for company. They are coming. Provide a place for them!

Leader, it is your responsibility to provide:

- A positive environment
- An element of fun
- An opportunity for involvement
- A clear message

Notes

Notes

16.

Teen Dating Is a Worldly Philosophy

Note: I saved this chapter for later in the book because I know this view of dating is not very popular.

Popular doesn't translate to mean right. God blesses righteous and isn't moved by man's opinion polls of what's deemed popular. Neither is God outdated or old-fashioned. His truth endureth to all generations.

God wants young people who embody his name and reflect his character. *Greater is He that is in you than he that is in the world. (1 John 4:4)*

Unless you want your 14-year-old having sex, babies or a premature marriage, you might want to reconsider the accepted worldview of dating.

Most people have bought into the worldview of teenage dating as a helpful social development that allows for a clearer understanding of what they want in a spouse. Although this may sound good, it is not faintly Biblical. Teenage dating as we know it today has existed for little more than 100 years. Courtship and marriage for centuries was overseen by parents who chose the marriage partner and made the marriage arrangements for their son or daughter.

Parents in most cases know more about what their offspring needs in a spouse than their son or daughter does. It's something to think about.

Young person, if your parents aren't happy with your choice for a mate, perhaps you should take a second look. It's worth consideration.

Biblical courtship is the pursuit of a spouse.

- Abraham sent his servant to pursue Rebekah as a spouse for Isaac.

- Boaz courted Ruth.

- Jacob pursued Rachel.

The struggle to balance sexual temptation and raging hormones with living a consistent Christian life is more pressure than a 15–year-old should have.

Teenagers aren't emotionally mature enough to handle the kind of dating society is confronting them with on a daily basis.

Worse than the pressure from peers is the pressure from ignorant parents pushing their young person into adult-like dating situations.

I was asked by a school teacher in my church to visit her class at the local junior high school. This class had 25 or more students ranging from 12 to 14 years old. She taught home economics. In this one class alone, there were 12 children expecting babies. The teacher told me she had other classes with a similar challenge.

Their teenage years were over. These young girls, as 12- to 14-year-old children, were faced with being moms or the murder of their unborn child through abortion. How do you think their underage pregnancy will affect their marriage possibilities?

That afternoon school visit made me hopping mad at the devil. This happened over 20 years ago and I'm still mad about it. This needless fiasco also makes me angry with ignorant parents who bought into the lie that their child is a good little boy or girl and more mature than those other young people.

Twelve- and fourteen-year-olds are not adults and do not have the capacity to function as mature adults.

That experience at the junior high school was an eye-opener for me. I began to initiate guidelines for how our young people should conduct themselves while under our care as a church ministry. Our church also began a Christian school the following fall.

While I was writing this section (2007), the morning news was on in another room and announced that one school in Massachusetts had 17 girls who had gotten pregnant as a pact among their social circle.

The oldest girl was only 16 years old. This was deliberate. It was planned.

It was reported that one girl got pregnant by a 24-year-old homeless man from a local homeless shelter. It was reported that this transpired with no romantic emotional ties. The man was just someone to get pregnant by.

71

Never in history has Satan initiated a more aggressive attack against our youth than is now being waged – and that includes his attempt at trying to kill Jesus as a baby. Satan means business. He's going for the kill. So should we. It probably should be noted that dating was introduced to the world (around 1900) at the same time God was fulfilling his promise of pouring out the Holy Spirit to this end-time generation. This insight is especially important in the light that every previous revival movement in history has had a crucial youth involvement. Satan has always introduced his version of "change" into the world for every revival movement in history.

Greater is he that is in you than he that is in the world. (I John 4:4)

By the way, my daughter and son are both very successful in business, in ministry and in marriage. *"The proof is in the pudding."* **These principles work!**

17.

God's Design

God created us male and female.

It's a natural reaction for a person to become sexually aroused when touching the body of the opposite sex. This is how God made people. This is how you got here. This is how I got here. This is why God also gave restraints for people to follow.

Kissing and heavy petting is a natural pathway to disaster when taken outside of marriage.

Teenagers will often make their boyfriend or girlfriend the most important thing in their life. God reserved this rite for mature marriage. God calls for our spouse to be the most important person to us. Teenagers cannot keep their romantic relationships from controlling their lives. They aren't emotionally mature enough to handle what is being pushed upon them. Teenagers commit suicide every year in larger and larger numbers. Many suicides are the result of a broken relationship the young person was too immature to handle. Mature adults in the church need to present the answers God has provided for our young people. It's high time for some Godly men and women to take a stand for our youth and not blink or back down.

One of the greatest hindrances to Christian growth among teenagers is teenage dating! You can quote me on that.

The true purpose of courtship is to find a spouse.

Teenage dating without a purpose (they certainly don't need a spouse) more often than not leads to sexual sin.

Those who are promiscuous as teenagers are seldom faithful as a marriage partner.

It's natural for young people to be attracted to the opposite sex. This is an emotion that comes at will when young people are around other young people of the opposite sex. We cannot control these emotions from happening, but we can control the opportunities for spending too much time together or allowing them to be alone.

Teenagers need safe opportunities to interact and enjoy each other's company without the pressure of dating.

Dating Rules That Work

Allow absolutely no physical contact between teenage boys and girls. Create the six-inch rule.

That's the rule that no one is to be closer than six inches from anyone. This also reduces scuffling among junior high guys.

Teenage girls and guys should not be allowed to sit together on the church bus or van or any other vehicle used to transport teenagers. The last two rows of the bus are reserved for all boys or all girls.

Whenever teenage dating becomes an issue, squelch it. There are some stupid parents that you may need to teach some Scriptures.

No couples are allowed to stay in their own little world in the youth group. Group participation creates a family atmosphere. Guys would never date their sister.

No swim parties with both guys and girls together. The guys might as well see the girls in their underwear and vice versa. Unless you are promoting lust and immorality, you will keep them separate for swim parties. We are trying to save a generation, not be popular. With television and Internet spitting out their satanic images of their brand of sexuality, the church must set a standard above reproach.

I know this is radical and certainly not popular. It will take radical young people to reach this generation. You will have more problems with parents on this issue than young people.

If you set this as a standard, pray for lots of wisdom to explain it to parents.

Cupid is not the youth pastor at your church. Cupid is not in charge. You are in charge!

Teenage guys will always be attracted to teenage girls and vice versa. We could never stop that and neither would we want to. What must be stopped are the disastrous opportunities the church blindly ignores where our young people are pressed into sexual temptations they aren't capable of controlling.

This includes long bus trips where guys and girls have their bodies pressed together in a bus seat for hours and often after dark. Think. And then think again.

The church cannot build a Joshua generation if their young people are destroyed by the devil while they are getting started.

18.

The Buddy System

Buddy commitments are the spiritual backbone of a successful youth ministry.

Iron sharpeneth iron: so a man sharpeneth the countenance of his friend. (Proverbs 27:17)

The buddy system will keep your teenagers from the dating temptation.

The buddy system is a verbal contract between two teenagers of the same sex to provide accountability for each other. This also allows for someone else be in a position of accounting for your life.

Your buddy must be someone who will be a friend who loves and trusts you at all times. Your buddy will stand by you when the going gets tough or when you are just sailing through on a cloud.

A friend loveth at all times. (Proverbs 17:17)

Your buddy will help you when the times of temptation come to pull you away from God's standards. You will care too much for your friend to let them backslide and vice versa.

Friends don't let friends go to Hell.

Having an accountability friend standing shoulder to shoulder with you will make the devil think twice about attacking you.

77

If your buddy sees anything in your life that doesn't look like Jesus, you want them to tell you about it.

Youth leaders, encourage your teenagers to be a part of a team of buddies who care and look out for each other's spiritual welfare. Just remember that friends who pull you down are not really friends. They are parasites.

This buddy system is kind of like the game of Red Rover where young people will lock their hands and arms together defying the opposing team to break through.

Two lines of young people would be formed about 30 feet apart. With their hands locked together, each team would take turns challenging the opposing team members to try to break through their line.

The battle cry was "Red Rover, Red Rover, we dare James (or Judy or any name on the opposing team) to come over." Then that person would charge the opposing team and attempt to break through. More often than not, the runner landed on the ground. They were then added to the opposing team. If they successfully broke through, they chose someone from the opposing team to add to their team.

The best strategy usually was to take the strongest member of your opposing team back to your team.

Another strategy often used in this game was to challenge the weaker members from the opposing team until the stronger members of the opposing team no longer had anyone to lock arms with.

I've seen a team with only one member left, standing to oppose everyone that had once been two equal opposing teams. This lone individual when challenged as the last member of his team would break through and one by one take all of his opposing team back and win the game. There is nothing impossible with God.

Young people standing shoulder-to-shoulder and locked arm-in-arm will not allow Satan to come over! This game is older than dirt but the concept still applies.

If you do not have a Christian buddy, pray and ask God for an accountability buddy who can stand with you to nudge and prod you to be more like Jesus so that Satan cannot break through. Your buddy helps keep you from getting off track and doing the wrong things. Every Christian young person should be encouraged to have a Christian accountability buddy. This is not a casual suggestion; it is an absolute imperative.

Over 90 percent of our Christian young people without an accountability buddy turn away from their faith when attending a secular college.

This statistic came to me from a major conservative denomination – the Southern Baptist.

Some of the devil's greatest advocates used to be faithful in Christian youth groups. Christian buddies are not an option! Parents and youth pastors would do well to discourage young people from going to a secular colleges and universities unless they have a Christian accountability buddy.

No position in life or person is worth going to Hell for.

Buddies should be committed to pray for each other every single day without exception. Every dream and fear needs to be shared with a Christian buddy as you would with God.

Again I say unto you, that if any two of you shall agree on earth as touching any thing that they shall ask, it shall be done for them of my father which is in heaven. (Matthew 18:19)

Whatever your age, you are not too young or old to have a Christian accountability buddy.

Do not be unequally yoked together with unbelievers. For what fellowship has righteousness with lawlessness? And what communion has light with darkness? And what accord has Christ with Belial? Or what part has a believer with an unbeliever? (2 Corinthians 6:14-15)

Swimming pool lifeguards have used the buddy system forever. We need to use it every day in our youth ministry. Someone needs to see that this generation is saved. Youth are drowning spiritually all around us. Teenagers need an accountability buddy.

Will that spiritual lifeguard be you?

Every Christian should have non-Christian friends but those you hang out with should provide Christian accountability.

Youth Buddy Covenant

- I will pray for my accountability partner every day.

- I will be accountable to my buddy concerning my daily Bible reading.

- I will honestly discuss any and all temptations that I am facing on a weekly basis.

- I will witness to someone at least once a week and share this report with my buddy.

- I covenant with my buddy to produce 12 younger disciples to follow this covenant by my senior year.

- I will be spiritually accountable to my youth pastor before God.

- I will conduct myself in a manner that pleases God.

Signed:_____

Signed:_____

Signed:_____

Discipleship with Purpose should be used as a companion manual to this book.

Endnotes

Chapter Three

1. Gallup Poll

Chapter Six

1. George Barna, *Ministry Currents 1*, no. 4 p.9

Chapter Thirteen

1. George Barna, *Ministry Currents 1*, no. 4 p.9

Chapter Twenty-three

1. Jack Hyles, *Pastors School*, First Baptist Church, Hammond, Indiana

Other Resources
By Anthony Fouts

Discipleship With Purpose

Perfect bound 86 pages

ISBN 978-0-9817391

Discipleship with a Purpose is a working manual to build strong Biblical character into the lives of believers. It is loaded with written-out Scripture for each section of discipleship. The three areas covered are **doctrine, disciplines and duplication**. This should be taught to every teenage class and to every new convert. Far too long the doctrines, disciplines and duplication of the Gospel have been neglected as a part of church health. Every leader in training should be taught the principles from Scripture contained in this manual.

Implementing Small Groups

Perfect bound 134 pages

ISBN 978-0-9817391-1-3

This book provides a simple guide for starting and maintaining effective small groups.

Implementing Small Groups gives an accurate Biblical and historical perspective to the modern church growth and provides a powerful tool for the 21st century church.

This practical guide to small group ministry is spelled out with clarity and a no-nonsense approach that gets to the heart of true community. *Implementing Small Groups* is a much-needed addition to any leader or pastor's library. It is a stand-alone capsule of straightforward information for starting and maintaining an active small group ministry.

Locating Your Harvest

Perfect bound 108 pages

ISBN 978-09817391-3-7

This is a book of eye-opening ideas to help churches in reaping their harvest.

Locating your Harvest is helping pastors all over America to recognize the harvest field God has provided in their own backyard. This is a book for pastors and church leaders who are sincere about reaching the harvest of souls that God has provided for them. It helps unveil the mystery of who your harvest may really be. This book will inspire you to find those people God has already prepared for your church.

Contact Us

For more information about
Church Growth Solutions or just talk to someone
about solutions for your ministry contact us at:

Postal Mail:

Church Growth Solutions
P.O. Box 744
Hutchins, Texas 75141

(note: Hutchins is a suburb of Dallas)

Email:

anthony@churchgrowthsolutions.com

Website:

www.ChurchGrowthSolutions.com

We are here for you!